ANIMALS IN ACTION
TEACHER'S GUIDE

Grades 5–9

Skills
Observing, Recording Data, Experimenting,
Making Inferences, Communicating

Concepts
Objective Observation, Animal Behavior,
Humaneness to Animals, Stimulus and Response

Themes
Systems & Interactions, Patterns of Change,
Diversity & Unity

Nature of Science and Mathematics
Objectivity & Ethics, Real-Life Applications, Scientific Community,
Cooperative Efforts, Creativity & Constraints,
Theory-Based and Testable

Time
Five 45-minute sessions
plus follow-up sessions

Katharine Barrett

Great Explorations in Math and Science (GEMS)
Lawrence Hall of Science
University of California at Berkeley

QL
751
.B1875
1991
c.2

Illustrations
Lisa Haderlie Baker
Carol Bevilacqua

Photographs
Reginald Barrett
Rose Craig
Saxon Donnelly

Lawrence Hall of Science, University of California, Berkeley, CA 94720. Chairman: Glenn T. Seaborg; Director: Marian C. Diamond

Publication was made possible by grants from the A. W. Mellon Foundation and the Carnegie Corporation of New York. This support does not imply responsibility for statements or views expressed in publications of the GEMS program. GEMS also gratefully acknowledges the contribution of word processing equipment from Apple Computer, Inc. Under a grant from the National Science Foundation, GEMS Leader's Workshops are being held across the country. For further information on GEMS leadership opportunities, please contact GEMS at the address and phone number below.

© 1986 by The Regents of the University of California. All rights reserved. Printed in the United States of America. Reprinted with revisions, 1991.

International Standard Book Number: 0-912511-10-9

COMMENTS WELCOME

Great Explorations in Math and Science (GEMS) is an ongoing curriculum development project. GEMS guides are revised periodically, to incorporate teacher comments and new approaches. We welcome your criticisms, suggestions, helpful hints, and any anecdotes about your experience presenting GEMS activities. Your suggestions will be reviewed each time a GEMS guide is revised. Please send your comments to: GEMS Revisions, c/o Lawrence Hall of Science, University of California, Berkeley, CA 94720. The telephone number is (415) 642-7771.

Great Explorations in Math and Science (GEMS) Program

The Lawrence Hall of Science (LHS) is a public science center on the University of California at Berkeley campus. LHS offers a full program of activities for the public, including workshops and classes, exhibits, films, lectures, and special events. LHS is also a center for teacher education and curriculum research and development.

Over the years, LHS staff have developed a multitude of activities, assembly programs, classes, and interactive exhibits. These programs have proven to be successful at the Hall and should be useful to schools, other science centers, museums, and community groups. A number of these guided-discovery activities have been published under the Great Explorations in Math and Science (GEMS) title, after an extensive refinement process that includes classroom testing of trial versions, modifications to ensure the use of easy-to-obtain materials, and carefully written and edited step-by-step instructions and background information to allow presentation by teachers without special background in mathematics or science.

Staff

Glenn T. Seaborg, Principal Investigator
Robert C. Knott, Administrator
Jacqueline Barber, Director
Cary Sneider, Curriculum Specialist
Rosita Fabian, Kimi Hosoume, Carolyn Willard,
    Staff Development Specialists
Cynthia Ashley, Administrative Coordinator
Gabriela Solomon, Distribution Coordinator
Lisa Haderlie Baker, Art Director
Carol Bevilacqua and Lisa Klofkorn, Designers
Lincoln Bergman and Kay Fairwell, Editors

Contributing Authors

Jacqueline Barber
Katharine Barrett
Lincoln Bergman
David Buller
Fern Burch
Deborah Calhoon
Linda De Lucchi
Jean Echols
Alan Gould
Sue Jacoda
Robert C. Knott
Larry Malone
Gay Nichols
Cary I. Sneider
Elizabeth Stage
Jennifer Meux White

Reviewers

We would like to thank the following educators who reviewed, tested, or coordinated the reviewing of this series of GEMS materials in manuscript form. Their critical comments and recommendations contributed significantly to these GEMS publications. Their participation does not necessarily imply endorsement of the GEMS program.

ALASKA
Olyn Garfield*
Galena City School, Galena

ARIZONA
Bill Armistead
Moon Mountain School, Phoenix
Flo-Ann Barwick
Lookout Mountain School, Phoenix
Richard E. Clark*
Washington School District, Phoenix
Bob Heath
Roadrunner School, Phoenix
Edie Helledy
Manzanita School, Phoenix
Greg Jesberger
Maryland School, Phoenix
Mark Kauppila
Acacia School, Phoenix
Karen Lee
Moon Mountain School, Phoenix
George Lewis
John Jacobs School, Phoenix
John Little
Palo Verde School, Phoenix
Tom Lutz
Palo Verde School, Phoenix
Tim Maki
Cactus Wren School, Phoenix
Don Metzler
Moon Mountain School, Phoenix
John O'Daniel
John Jacobs School, Phoenix
Donna Pickering
Orangewood School, Phoenix
Brenda Pierce
Cholla School, Phoenix
Ken Redfield
Washington School, Phoenix
Jean Reinoehl
Alta Vista School, Phoenix
Liz Sandberg
Desert Foothills School, Phoenix
Sandy Stanley
Manzanita School, Phoenix
Charri Strong
Lookout Mountain School, Phoenix
Shirley Vojtko
Cholla School, Phoenix

CALIFORNIA
Bob Alpert*
Vista School, Albany
Karen Ardito
White Hill Junior High School, Fairfax
James Boulier
Dan Mini Elementary School, Vallejo
Susan Butsch
Albany Middle School, Albany
Susan Chan
Cornell School, Albany
Robin Davis
Albany Middle School, Albany
Claudia Hall
Horner Junior High School, Fremont
Dale Kerstad*
Cave Elementary School, Vallejo
Joanna Klaseen
Albany Middle School, Albany
Margaret Lacrampe
Sleepy Hollow School, Orinda
Linda McClanahan*
Horner Junior High School, Fremont
Tina Neivelt
Cave Elementary School, Vallejo
Neil Nelson
Cave Elementary School, Vallejo
Mark Piccillo
Frick Junior High School, Oakland
Cindy Plambeck
Albany Middle School, Albany
Susan Power
Albany Middle School, Albany
Carol Rutherford
Cave Elementary School, Vallejo
Jim Salak
Cave Elementary School, Vallejo
Rich Salisbury
Albany Middle School, Albany
Secondo Sarpieri*
Vallejo City Unified School District, Vallejo
Bob Shogren*
Albany Middle School, Albany
Theodore L. Smith
Frick Junior High School, Oakland
Kay Sorg
Albany Middle School, Albany
Bonnie Square
Cave Elementary School, Vallejo
Jack Thornton*
Dan Mini Elementary School, Vallejo
Alice Tolinder*
Vallejo City Unified School District, Vallejo
Pamela Zimmerman
Cornell School, Albany

KENTUCKY
Mary Artner
Adath Jeshurun Preschool, Louisville
Alice Atchley
Wheatley Elementary School, Louisville
Sandi Babbitz
Adath Jeshurun Preschool, Louisville
Phyl Breuer
Holy Spirit School, Louisville
Toni Davidson
Thomas Jefferson Middle School, Louisville
August Drufke
Museum of History and Science, Louisville
Riva Drutz
Adath Jeshurun Preschool, Louisville
Linda Erman
Adath Jeshurun Preschool, Louisville
Jennie Ewalt
Adath Jeshurun Preschool, Louisville
Sam Foster
Museum of History and Science, Louisville
Nancy Glaser
Thomas Jefferson Middle School, Louisville
Laura Hansen
Sacred Heart Model School, Louisville
Leo Harrison
Thomas Jefferson Middle School, Louisville
Muriel Johnson
Thomas Jefferson Middle School, Louisville
Pam Laveck
Sacred Heart Model School, Louisville
Amy S. Lowen*
Museum of History and Science, Louisville
Theresa H. Mattei*
Museum of History and Science, Louisville
Brad Matthews
Jefferson County Public Schools, Louisville
Cathy Maddox
Thomas Jefferson Middle School, Louisville
Sherrie Morgan
Prelude Preschool, Louisville
Sister Mary Mueller
Sacred Heart Model School, Louisville
Tony Peake
Brown School, Louisville
Ann Peterson
Adath Jeshurun Preschool, Louisville
Mike Plamp
Museum of History and Science, Louisville
John Record
Thomas Jefferson Middle School, Louisville
Susan Reigler
St. Francis High School, Louisville
Anne Renner
Wheatley Elementary School, Louisville
Ken Rosenbaum
Jefferson County Public Schools, Louisville
Edna Schoenbaechler
Museum of History and Science, Louisville
Melissa Shore
Museum of History and Science, Louisville
Joan Stewart
DuPont Manual Magnet School, Louisville
Jenna Stinson
Thomas Jefferson Middle School, Louisville
Dr. William M. Sudduth*
Museum of History and Science, Louisville
Larry Todd
Brown School, Louisville
Harriet Waldman
Adath Jeshurun Preschool, Louisville
Fife Scobie Wicks
Museum of History and Science, Louisville
August Zoeller
Museum of History and Science, Louisville
Doris Zoeller
Museum of History and Science, Louisville

MICHIGAN
Dave Bierenga
South Christian School, Kalamazoo
Edgar Bosch
South Christian School, Kalamazoo
Craig Brueck
Schoolcraft Middle School, Schoolcraft
Joann Dehring
Woodland Elementary School, Portage
Tina Echols
Lincoln Elementary School, Kalamazoo
Barbara Hannaford
Gagie School, Kalamazoo
Dr. Alonzo Hannaford*
Science and Mathematics Education Center
Western Michigan University, Kalamazoo
Rita Hayden*
Science and Mathematics Education Center
Western Michigan University, Kalamazoo
Mary Beth Hunter
Woodland Elementary School, Portage

Ruth James
Portage Central High School, Portage
Dr. Phillip T. Larsen*
Science and Mathematics Education Center
Western Michigan University, Kalamazoo
Gloria Lett*
Kalamazoo Public Schools, Kalamazoo
Roslyn Ludwig
Woodland Elementary School, Portage
David McDill
Harper Creek High School, Battle Creek
Everett McKee
Woodland Elementary School, Portage
Susie Merrill
Gagie School, Kalamazoo
Rick Omilian*
Science and Mathematics Education Center
Western Michigan University, Kalamazoo
Kathy Patton
Northeastern Elementary School, Kalamazoo
Rebecca Penney
Harper Creek High School, Battle Creek
Shirley Pickens
Schoolcraft Elementary School, Schoolcraft
Deb Ply
South Junior High School, Kalamazoo
Sue Schell
Gagie School, Kalamazoo
Sharon Schillaci
Schoolcraft Elementary School, Schoolcraft
Julie Schmidt
Gagie School, Kalamazoo
Joel Schuitema
Woodland Elementary School, Portage
Bev Wrubel
Woodland Elementary School, Portage

NEW YORK
Frances Bargamian
Trinity Elementary School, New Rochelle
Bob Broderick
Trinity Elementary School, New Rochelle
Richard Golden*
Webster Magnet Elementary School, New Rochelle
Tom Mullen
Jefferson Elementary School, New Rochelle
Edna Neita
George M. Davis Elementary School, New Rochelle
Sigrin Newell
Discovery Center, Albany
Eileen Paolicelli
Ward Elementary School, New Rochelle
Dr. John V. Pozzi*
City School District of New Rochelle, New Rochelle
John Russo
Ward Elementary School, New Rochelle
Bruce Seiden
Webster Magnet Elementary School, New Rochelle
David Selleck
Albert Leonard Junior High School, New Rochelle
Tina Sudak
Ward Elementary School, New Rochelle
Julia Taibi
George M. Davis Elementary School, New Rochelle
Rubye Vester
Columbus Elementary School, New Rochelle
Bruce Zeller
Isaac E. Young Junior High School, New Rochelle

NORTH CAROLINA
Jorge Escobar
North Carolina Museum of Life and Science, Durham
Ed Gray
Discovery Place, Charlotte
Sue Griswold
Discovery Place, Charlotte
Mike Jordan
Discovery Place, Charlotte
James D. Keighton*
North Carolina Museum of Life and Science, Durham
Paul Nicholson
North Carolina Museum of Life and Science, Durham
John Paschal
Discovery Place, Charlotte
Cathy Preiss
Discovery Place, Charlotte
Carol Sawyer
Discovery Place, Charlotte
Patricia J. Wainland*
Discovery Place, Charlotte

OHIO
A.M. Sarquis
Miami University, Middletown

OREGON
Christine Bellavita
Judy Cox
David Heil*
Shab Levy
Joanne McKinley
Catherine Mindolovich
Margaret Noone*
Jim Todd
Ann Towsley
Oregon Museum of Science and Industry

Oregon Museum of Science and Industry (OMSI) staff conducted trial tests at the following sites:
Berean Child Care Center, Portland
Grace Collins Memorial Center, Portland
Mary Rieke Talented and Gifted Center,
   Portland Public School District, Portland
Portland Community Center, Portland
Portland Community College, Portland
St. Vincent De Paul, Child Development
   Center, Portland
Salem Community School, Salem
Volunteers of America, Child Care Center,
   Portland

WASHINGTON
David Foss
Stuart Kendall
Dennis Schatz*
William C. Schmitt
David Taylor
Pacific Science Center, Seattle

FINLAND
Sture Björk
Åbo Akademi, Vasa
Arja Raade
Katajanokka Elementary School, Helsinki
Pirjo Tolvanen
Katajanokan Ala-Aste, Helsinki
Gloria Weng*
Katajanokka Elementary School, Helsinki

*Trial test coordinators

Contents

Acknowledgments viii
Introduction.. 1
Background 3
Session 1: The Animal Corral 5
Session 2: Stimulus and Response................. 11
Session 3: Small Critters in Action................. 17
Session 4: Team Experiments....................... 25
Session 5: Scientific Convention 29
Going Further.. 31
Small Animal Resource Guide 33
Where To Get Live Critters 42
Code of Practice on Use of Animals in Schools... 43
References.. 44
Summary Outlines....................................45

Acknowledgments

We would like to thank the following members of the Lawrence Hall of Science Biology staff for their helpful comments and suggestions on the drafts of this publication: Gigi Dornfest, Alisya Galo, and Jefferey Kaufmann.

Introduction

"The hamster's stuffing seeds in its pouch!" "The cricket's dodging the chick!" "The rat's climbing the branch!" In this unit, your students investigate the patterns and puzzles of behavior by observing animals in action.

The activity begins with students seated around a large classroom corral containing a lively young animal, such as a gerbil. Students take turns describing how the animal explores the open space. Then they observe another animal and are introduced to the concepts of objective observation, behavior, anthropomorphism, and humane treatment of animals.

On another day, students explore the concepts of stimulus and response by adding foods, shelters, and other objects to the corral and observing how each animal reacts. They also discuss how certain behaviors might help wild animals survive.

Students then conduct their own research by observing the behavior of common small animals such as crayfish, isopods, ladybugs, crickets, guppies, or garden snails. The unit concludes with a simulated scientific convention during which students discuss their findings and suggest ways their experiments could be improved.

This introduction to observing and experimenting can assist your students in planning and conducting their own Science Fair research projects.

Background

The Process of Experimenting

The intent of this unit is to introduce students to the process of experimenting while allowing them to exercise their curiosity about animals. Students first learn and apply basic concepts about scientific observation. They observe animal behavior, add various stimuli, and note reactions. This prepares the way for students to design some initial experiments.

Of course, it is not possible to control all the factors that might influence the outcome of an animal behavior experiment under classroom conditions; your students are unlikely to achieve a finely-controlled test situation. They will, however, be able to learn more about animal behavior, and will gain valuable experience in applying and refining the critical thinking skills needed in scientific experimentation.

People often have a tendency to ascribe human characteristics to animals. This type of description is called an *anthropomorphism.* Why does a young chicken peck at its image in a mirror? Students often reply, "It's checking to see how it looks."

Your students will need many reminders that their explanations should be based on *observations* (the gerbil ran around the corral) so as to avoid jumping to anthropomorphic conclusions (the gerbil likes to exercise).

Humane Treatment of Animals

Teachers and students who demonstrate responsible behavior toward animals can have a strong positive influence as role models on those students who have had less contact with animals. For this reason, we recommend that your entire class be involved in the planning and preparation of the animal investigations. Every student should have a chance to practice humane procedures while holding and caring for the animals.

A "Code of Practice on Use of Animals in Schools," recommended by the National Science Teachers Association, is included in this booklet. You may want to refer to these guidelines before beginning these sessions. The code of practice is reprinted on page 43.

Session 1: The Animal Corral

Overview

Behavior includes all the ways an animal reacts to changes in its external or internal environment. Sniffing and scratching are examples of behaviors that are an animal's response to its environment.

The animal corral is a stimulating arena for lively animals. Your students will enjoy describing and comparing the ways different animals explore the new environment. Young animals make the best subjects because they tend to be more active and to explore new surroundings. Also, students are less fearful of young animals.

Time Frame

Observing Animals	20 minutes
More Observations	15 minutes
Humane Treatment of Animals	10 minutes

What You Need

For the group:
- ☐ 6 or 7 cardboard boxes about 18" x 18" x 24" (45 cm x 45 cm x 60 cm)
- ☐ 1 sharp knife
- ☐ 1 roll of strong tape for linking the cut-open boxes together to form a corral
- ☐ 2 or 3 young active animals, preferably ones that can get along together in the corral (*small* pets from home work well—no large dogs or adult cats.)
- ☐ cages, bedding, and food for the animals*
- ☐ newspapers or drop cloths to put under the corral if your classroom is carpeted
- ☐ paper towels, soap, and water for cleaning up
- ☐ chalkboard and chalk
- ☐ 1 large piece of butcher paper
- ☐ 1 large marking pen

Litters of hamsters, gerbils, rats, guinea pigs, kittens, rabbits, and young chicks make interesting subjects. Rats, guinea pigs, and rabbits are often compatible in the same corral.

*Refer to *Creatures in the Classroom* (1976) for guidelines on care, housing, and experiments appropriate to the various animals. See References, page 44, for further information on this excellent sourcebook.

Getting Ready

1. Refer to the section on humane procedures, page 43.

2. With assistance from your students, arrange transportation, housing, and care for several animals. Ask for volunteers to feed and take care of the animals.

3. Organize an area of the classroom where the animals and supplies can be kept.

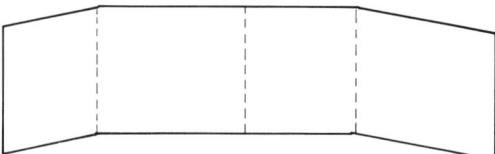

4. Make the animal corral by removing the tops and bottoms from about six large boxes. Open the sides of each box to make a long panel. Tape the panels together to form a large rectangular corral about 8 x 12 feet (2.5 x 3.5 meters). To save time, a long table turned on its side, or a wall of the room, can serve as part of the corral.

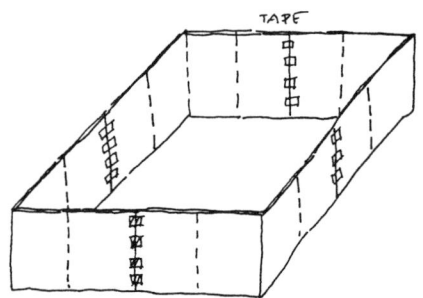

5. Set up the corral in view of the chalkboard. If your classroom is carpeted, use a drop cloth or newspaper to protect the floor.

Animal Observations

1. Ask the students to arrange their chairs around the outside of the corral and sit down. Once your students are seated, pick up the animal you plan to begin with so everyone can see how you handle it in a gentle way. Point out that the animal is much smaller than they are and can be hurt or scared if students are not careful and quiet.

2. Explain that the term *behavior* is used to include **everything** an animal does. Each animal has a variety of ways of reacting to its environment. The sum of these actions makes up its behavior. Tell the students they will have a few minutes to watch the animal's actions in the corral.

This should be a relaxed, enjoyable time that can be extended if the animal's actions are varied and interesting.

3. Ask a student volunteer to place the animal in the corral. Encourage the students to take turns quietly describing what the animal does, so the entire class can hear the vocabulary used to describe the various actions.

4. After about five minutes, remove the animal from the corral and return it to its cage.

5. While the students are still seated around the corral, write the heading "Observations" at the top of the chalkboard, and ask the students what the term means. If the students don't suggest it, tell them that an observation is based on something they can see, hear, smell, feel, or taste. Ask them what senses they used to observe the animal in the corral.

6. Invite the students to report their observations; list five to ten of these on the chalkboard under the kind of animal you used. Accept all of their descriptions even if some are not direct observations. (See "Observations" chart.)

7. Then deliberately insert an *assumption* of your own, such as, "the animal wants to get out." Point out that this is your idea or assumption about why the animal is acting that way, **not** a direct observation.

8. Erase the assumption and ask the students to replace it with an observed action, such as, "it jumped up on the wall," or "it scratched in the corner."

9. Ask the students to check the list to see if the other entries are direct observations based on information from their senses. Put parentheses around entries that are **not** observations.

10. Introduce the word **anthropomorphism**. People often assume that animals have the same feelings and motives as we do.

   Give an example of anthropomorphism and ask students to suggest other examples. Point out that we cannot "see" into the mind of an animal to find out how it feels or thinks.

   Remind students to base their conclusions on **observations,** not on what they themselves might feel in the same situation.

Most animals will eventually urinate or defecate in the corral. Point out that this is a natural and important behavior. Many animals (dogs, cats, mice) use urine as an "I was here" message to other animals.

```
              OBSERVATIONS
GERBIL                    GUINEA PIG
HOPS ALONG WALL           HOLDS STILL
SNIFFS AIR                TURNS HEAD
HOPS TO CORNER            WALKS TO WALL
(WANTS TO GET OUT)        WALKS ALONG WALL
SCRATCHES IN CORNER       SQUEAKS
GOES TO BRANCH            (IS AFRAID)
NIBBLES BRANCH            WALKS TO FOOD
                          NIBBLES APPLE
```

Examples of Assumptions:

It's looking for food.
It wants to go to sleep.
It's sick.
It wants its mother.

Examples of Anthropomorphism:

It's fooling around.
It wants to go on a diet.
It's unhappy and doesn't want to play.
It misses its friends.

More Observations

1. Ask a volunteer to add a new animal to the corral. Encourage the students to quietly describe the actions of this animal.

2. Remove the animal from the corral and direct the group's attention to the "Observations" chart.

3. Begin a new list under the name of the second animal, and record five to ten of the students' observations.

4. Ask the class, "Are any of these new entries *anthropomorphisms* or *assumptions*?" Check over the lists with them to make certain that all descriptions are based on direct observations.

5. If the two animals are compatible, put them together in the corral for a few more minutes so students can observe the interactions.

6. Ask questions to stimulate more comparisons, such as: "What actions of both animals were similar? What behaviors of the two animals were different? Where in the corral did the animals spend the most time?"

7. In the course of this discussion, students will tend to draw conclusions. In each case, have the class check to make sure that the conclusion is based on direct observations. Point out that many people have a tendency to jump to conclusions, so it is important to make accurate and careful observations before assessing final results.

8. Students who handled the animals should wash their hands with soap and water.

9. Tell the class that in the next session they will explore animal responses to objects added to the corral environment. Ask for volunteers to bring a variety of materials from home, such as foods, shelters, toys, and other objects for the animals to investigate. Caution the class to avoid materials that could harm the animals.

Humane Treatment of Animals

1. Tell the class there are laws protecting animals. Ask, "Why do you suppose people have to make these laws?"

2. Introduce the term *humane*, and ask the students how they can be humane to the classroom animals. List their responses on a large sheet of paper. This list can become part of class guidelines for humane treatment. (See page 31, Going Further).

Vocabulary Check

Anthropomorphism: the attribution of human characteristics to an animal.

Assumption: a conclusion that is not based on direct sensory observation; something that is assumed but not proven.

Behavior: everything an animal does, all the ways it reacts to changes in its environment.

Conclusion: a judgment or decision formed after investigation. To jump to conclusions is to decide before making observations; to make up one's mind before facts and circumstances are sufficiently known.

Humane: showing kindness, compassion, and consideration for humans and animals.

Objective: to be objective is to base one's viewpoint on observations from the external world rather than on assumptions.

Observation: the process of noting an occurrence through sight, smell, sound, touch, or taste.

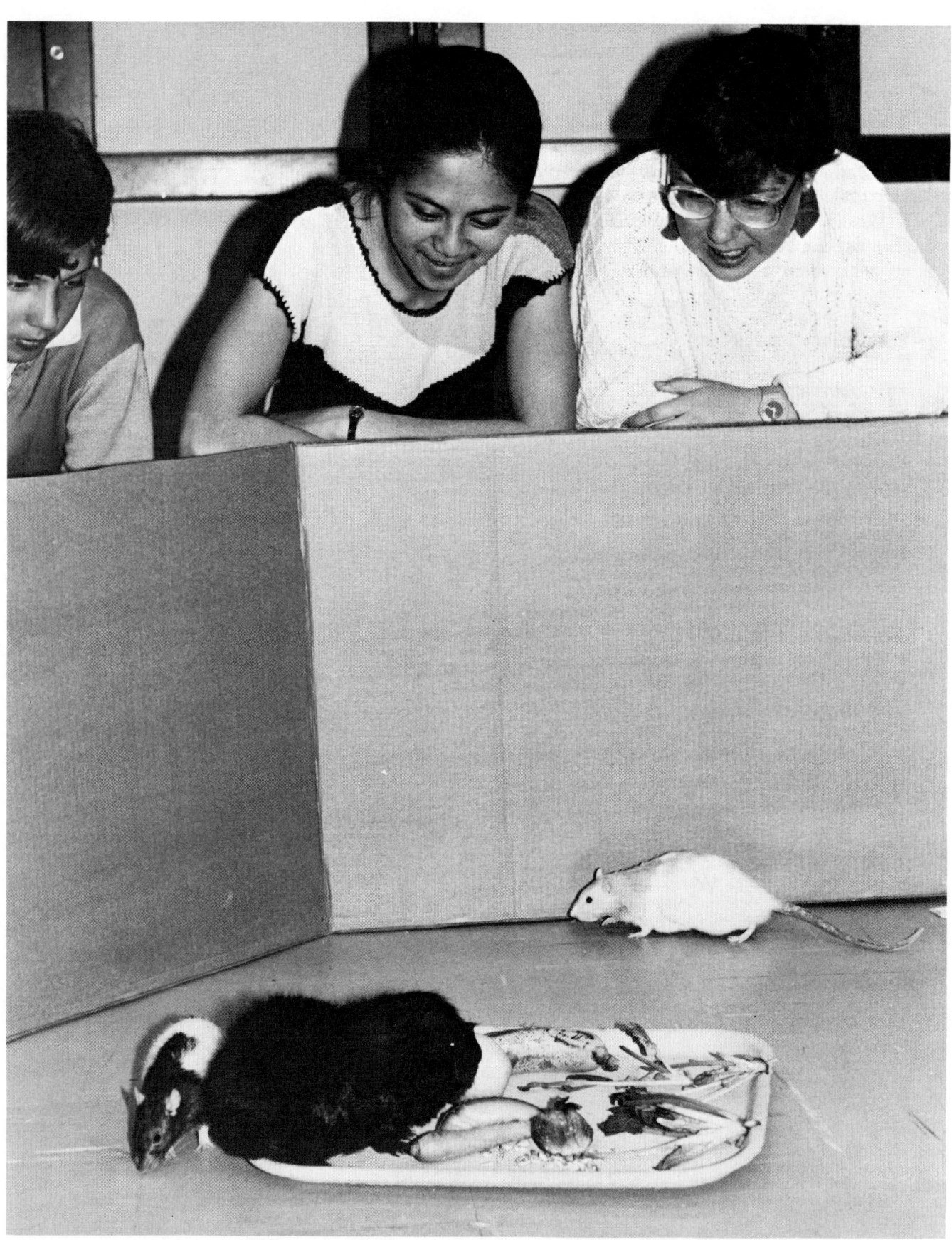

10　Session 2

Session 2: Stimulus and Response

Overview

There are reasons why animals behave as they do. When an animal does something, it is reacting to a *stimulus* from its external or internal environment. In this activity, your students introduce stimulus objects, such as foods, into an animal's environment and observe how the animal reacts. Students then learn what a hypothesis is and generate hypotheses about how certain behaviors help wild animals survive.

Time Frame

Stimulus/Response — 30 minutes
Discussing Behavior — 15 minutes

What You Need

- [ ] 1 large corral
- [ ] 2–3 active animals
- [ ] cage, bedding, and food for the animals
- [ ] a wide variety of objects to add to the corral, such as foods, branches, a tray of soil, shelters, toys, yarn, mirrors, sponges soaked with peppermint or vanilla extract, etc.
- [ ] 4–6 large pieces of butcher paper for recording the group's observations
- [ ] 1 large marking pen
- [ ] tape
- [ ] newspapers or drop cloths to put under the corral
- [ ] paper towels, soap, water for cleanup

Getting Ready

1. Prepare data charts with the headings "Object or Stimulus" and "Observed Response" on large sheets of paper for *each animal* you plan to observe. Tape the charts to the wall where they can be seen from the corral area. These charts should provide more space than the chalkboard, and can be saved for use in future activities.

2. Set up the corral, and arrange the stimulus objects where the class can easily see the variety of items.

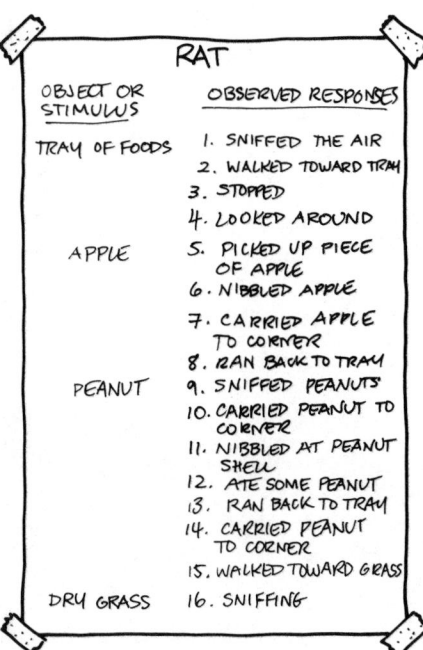

Stimulus and Response

1. Have the students sit on chairs around the outside of the corral. Tell them they will be working like a team of biologists observing how an animal reacts to changes in its environment.

2. Introduce the concepts of *stimulus* and *response* in the following manner. Suddenly make a loud noise or do something unusual to surprise the group (drop a book or shout). Ask several students how they reacted when you made the loud noise.

A *stimulus* is anything to which an organism reacts. In this case, the stimulus was the loud noise.

A *response* is how an organism reacts to a stimulus. In this case, the response was the students' surprised reactions to the loud noise.

3. Ask the students to look at the corral environment and name *all of the stimuli* that might cause an animal to respond [corral, floor, people, smells, temperature, noises].

4. Show the students objects that may be put in the corral as additional stimuli. Explain that they will observe and describe the animals' responses to each stimulus as it is placed into the corral.

5. Ask a volunteer to place one animal in the corral. Encourage students to take turns quietly describing the animal's actions for several minutes.

6. Let the class choose which stimulus they would like to try first, and have a volunteer add the object to the corral. List the students' observations on the chart.

7. Select other students to add new objects to the corral, one at a time. Observe the animal's response to each object for several minutes before removing it and adding a different object. After about 10 minutes ask a volunteer to remove the animal from the corral.

8. Ask, "How did the animal respond to the volunteer? What stimulus attracted the animal the most? What qualities of this object might have attracted the animal?"

9. Have volunteers remove the stimulus object from the corral and add another animal. Repeat the stimulus/response tests for the new animal, and record the students' observations on the appropriate data charts.

10. If the animals are compatible, return the first animal to the corral and have the students describe the interactions between the two for a few minutes.

Discussion

1. Direct the students' attention to the data, and ask them to compare the actions of the two animals.

2. Encourage individuals to share their ideas and knowledge about the possible benefit of certain actions to a wild animal. Ask, "Can anyone give examples of ways a wild animal behaves that help it to survive?" "How might a wild rat benefit from running along walls instead of across open spaces?"

3. During the discussion, point out that it is often difficult to identify which stimuli cause certain behaviors, and to determine the exact use or value of the responses to the animal.

When biologists study animals, they often come up with ideas to explain why the animal acts the way it does. They use these ideas to make a more formal *hypothesis* or statement which can then be investigated.

Guide the students in generating hypotheses to explain the behavior of some animals. For example:

"Wolves often howl at night. What ideas do you have to explain that behavior?" [They are hungry; they are trying to locate another wolf, etc.]

"What's an example of a hypothesis?" [Hungry wolves howl more than wolves that are well-fed.]

"The rat we observed carried three peanuts from the center of the corral to the corner. What hypothesis might relate to that behavior?" [If rats are given food in an open space they will move the food to a sheltered area.]

4. Ask, "How could you study the behavior of a wild animal such as a wolf?" "How could you keep track of your observations?" [Take pictures or movies of animals. Keep a journal. Follow the animal and its tracks. Use binoculars to watch the animal. Use radio collars to locate and follow the animals, etc.]

5. Conclude the discussion by telling students they will conduct their own investigations of animal behavior in future sessions.

Vocabulary Check

Hypothesis: an idea or proposed explanation about natural phenomena to be tested or proved through observation and experiment.

Response: something an animal does in reaction to a stimulus.

Stimulus: something an animal detects through its senses.

Session 3: Small Critters in Action

Overview

During this session, students observe a small organism exploring an environment containing a variety of stimuli. You should select the species you want the students to observe **at least two weeks in advance** of this session, to allow time for ordering and/or collecting the organisms.

This activity involves some review of concepts used in the previous two sessions. This reinforcement should prove helpful to your students as they frame their own hypotheses and design original experiments. After the students explore the responses of small organisms to stimuli, you then guide them through the process of planning an experiment.

During the planning process, you may wish to introduce the concept of a *fair test*, or controlled experiment, as briefly described alongside the Planning Experiments heading on page 20. You may also wish to refer to the "Small Animal Resource Guide," beginning on page 33, for sample questions to investigate. However, these questions are only examples and suggestions, and are in no way meant to discourage the originality and creativity of your students, who are likely to come up with lots of great questions on their own.

Time Frame

Describing Actions	20 minutes
Discussing Observations	5 minutes
Planning Experiments	20 minutes

What You Need

Have your students assist you in obtaining these materials. **It is important that all teams observe the same species of animal.**

For each team of four students:
- ☐ 2 animals of the same species (e.g., guppies, crayfish, milkweed bugs, isopods, crickets, mealworms, beetles, butterfly larvae, garden snails). See "Small Animal Resource Guide," page 33, for brief descriptions of the care and feeding of these animals.
- ☐ 1 animal observation container
- ☐ food and water for the animals
- ☐ objects to be used as stimuli in the behavior experiments (see sidebars for suggestions)
- ☐ sponge or paper towels, and water for cleanup
- ☐ 1 team record sheet "Animal Behavior Experiment" (master included, page 23)

For each student:
- ☐ 1 student observation sheet, "Observing Animal Behavior" (master included, page 22)
- ☐ 1 clipboard or book to use as a writing surface

Observation Containers: Plastic sweater boxes, plastic dish tubs, metal baking pans, shoe boxes, milk cartons, and small aquaria make suitable observation chambers for behavior experiments with small animals.

Getting Ready

1. If you plan to obtain organisms from a biological supply house, place your order **three to four weeks ahead of time.** Your students may be able to assist you by collecting and making cages for isopods, garden snails, crayfish, butterfly larvae, and crickets.

2. Make copies of the student observation sheet, "Observing Animal Behavior," and of the team

2. Make copies of the student observation sheet, "Observing Animal Behavior," and of the team record sheet, "Animal Behavior Experiment," found on pages 22 and 23.

3. Just before class, put one or two animals in each of the observation containers to be used by the teams.

Describing Actions

1. Tell the students they will be investigating the behavior of a small organism. Ask a volunteer to redefine the term *behavior*.

2. Introduce the animals and explain where you got them. *Avoid giving the students information they can discover through their own investigations.*

3. Tell students they will use a similar procedure to the one used in the Animal Corral activity. They will add stimulus objects to the animal's container and observe how the animal responds.

4. Distribute copies of the student observation sheet ("Observing Animal Behavior") and the clipboards. Point out that each person will make his or her own record of observations.

5. Divide the class into teams of four students, and review the stimulus objects that may be used with the animals.

6. Tell the students to introduce one stimulus at a time into the observation container. Ask them to carefully observe and record the animal's responses. Remind the students that the small organisms should be treated with respect and humaneness.

7. Give each team a container with one or two animals, and mention that the teams will have about 15 minutes to test the animal's responses to the stimulus objects.

8. After about 15 minutes, collect the containers and animals.

Stimuli and Objects to Use with Terrestrial Animals:

different colors of paper
different colors of flowers
hairy leaves, smooth leaves
smelly plants (mint, eucalyptus, onions, garlic)
variety of foods
straws for blowing air
tuning forks for sounds
smooth and textured surfaces
slanted surfaces
spray from water bottle
wet and dry sand or soil
heating pad
branches
shelters
flashlight
other animals of same species

Stimuli and Objects to Use with Aquatic Animals:

clean pebbles and rocks
plastic flower pots
water plants
small shiny objects
plastic straws for blowing bubbles
mirrors
string or thread
small insects
cotton soaked in foods
flashlight with colored filters
other animals of same species

Discussing Observations

1. Ask the students to report on which objects or stimuli seem to influence their animal's behavior. List the stimuli and responses on the board.

2. Referring to the list of observations, ask, "Are any of these entries **anthropomorphisms** or **assumptions**?" Have the students check their own lists to make certain that all descriptions are **observations**.

Planning Experiments

1. Tell the group you are going to help them design an animal behavior experiment. Guide them through the following steps:

   a. Choose one of the stimuli that was used with the animals (e.g., food, shelter, color). Think of a topic to investigate. For example: "Let's suppose we want to find out if crickets prefer one color."

   b. Narrow the topic to one idea or **hypothesis** that can be tested within a period of 25 minutes. For example: "Crickets will prefer dark brown over light tan."

   c. Identify the choices available to the animal in this experiment. For example: "Crickets will be given a choice of two colors of paper on the bottom of their cage: tan and dark brown."

   d. Identify the actions you will observe and record. For example: "We will record how much time the cricket spends sitting on each color."

   e. Describe how you will attempt to make your experiment a *fair test* so only the test stimulus influences your animal. For example: "We will make the colored papers the same size, and we will cover the box with clear plastic to keep wind and noise from disturbing the animals."

A Fair Test

Here is an example of a fair test: Suppose you want to compare two kinds of soil to see which grows the taller plants. You need to make sure the plant seeds are the same variety, receive the same amount of water, and are placed in the same sunlight. This allows the type of soil to vary (to be a "variable"), while keeping the other growth factors constant or "controlled."

Although working with animals in a classroom does not allow the same strict control, the idea of a fair test can be communicated and approximated. Even very young students have encountered concepts of "fairness," and this can be used as a starting point for discussions of controlled experiments.

2. Choosing a realistic topic and making a clear plan are crucial steps in conducting an experiment. Often students are tempted to bypass the design stages in their eagerness to get on with the action. Emphasize the importance of careful advance planning in designing an experiment.

3. Suggest other experiments that could be conducted. You may wish to refer to the questions to investigate in the "Small Animal Resource Guide." You may also want to list several variables on the chalkboard for students to choose from: light/dark, moist/dry, warm/cold, rough/smooth, flat/slanted.

4. Distribute the "Animal Behavior Experiment" sheets, and encourage the teams to spend about ten minutes planning their experiments and filling out the first two items on the record sheet.

5. Wrap up the session by asking one or two teams to describe and discuss their plans with the rest of the class. Encourage the students to give each other constructive suggestions for improving the design of their experiments.

6. Collect the team plans and review them before the next session. Some plans may be hazardous for the animals or too complex to control. Add your own comments and questions to encourage the teams to modify and improve their designs.

Vocabulary Check

Fair Test: an experiment designed to provide a valid or "fair" measure or comparison during a scientific investigation; a controlled experiment. The factor being investigated is compared, while other factors that might influence the outcome are kept constant or "controlled."

NAME: _____

OBSERVING ANIMAL BEHAVIOR

Name of Animal: _____

List the stimuli you used and the animal's responses:

Object or Stimulus	Response

RECORDER: _____
OTHER TEAM MEMBERS: _____
_____
_____

ANIMAL BEHAVIOR EXPERIMENT

Name of Animal:

1. What is your hypothesis?

2. Describe your experiment:

3. Record your observations:

4. What are your conclusions?

5. How did you make sure the experiment was a **fair test?**

6. Ideas for improving the experiment:

7. On the back of this paper sketch your experimental setup.

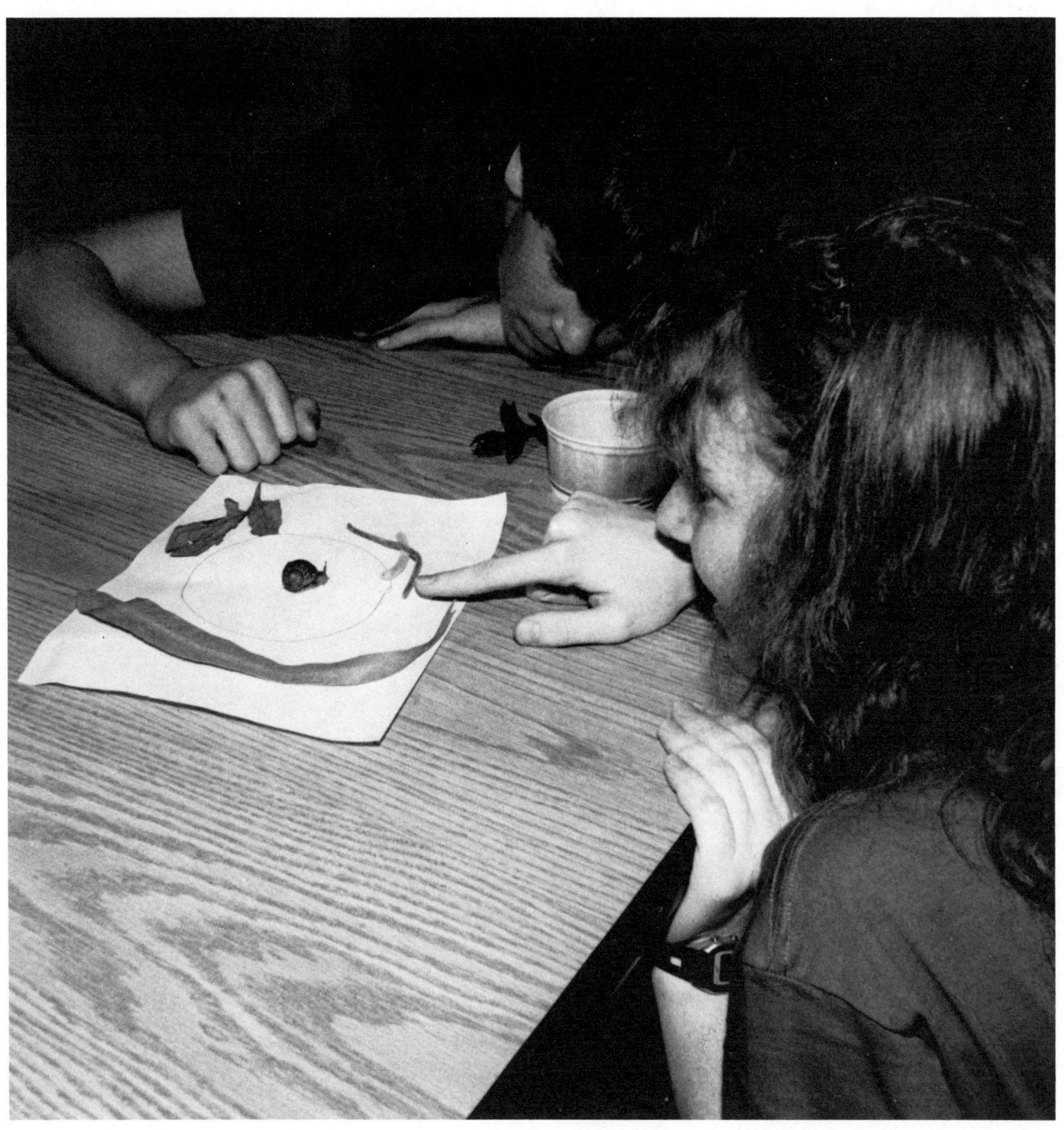

Session 4: Team Experiments

Overview

In this session, the students will conduct and evaluate their own animal behavior experiments.

Time Frame

Getting Started   10 minutes
Experimenting   25 minutes
Analyzing the Results   10 minutes

What You Need

For each team of four students:
- ☐ the team record sheet, "Animal Behavior Experiment" (master included, page 23)
- ☐ animals and equipment from previous session
- ☐ sponge or paper towels, and water for cleanup

Getting Ready

1. Review each team's plan for the behavior experiment.

2. Make certain that animals and equipment are organized and easily accessible to the students.

 ### Getting Started

1. Stress the need for teamwork in getting materials together and experiments set up. Tell the teams to:

- select a person who will serve as a Recorder
- select a Materials Manager
- select an Animal Manager
- select an Assistant Animal Manager

2. Return the "Animal Behavior Experiment" sheets to the team Recorders. Remind students that all team members share responsibility for assisting the Recorder in making an accurate report of observations.

3. Tell the teams to get their materials and set up their experiments. You may have to arbitrate inter-team competition for space and materials. Notify them that there is a 25-minute time limit for the experiments.

Experimenting

1. Circulate among the teams as they work, lending assistance as needed. Encourage students to be as precise as possible in describing what happens in their experiments.

2. Remind the students to avoid interfering with the animals during their experiment. Point out the need for giving the animals a few minutes to respond to the stimulus that is being tested.

3. About midway through the period, remind the teams of the time limit. Stress the importance of recording **all** the results, not just the ones that seem to fit their hypotheses.

Analyzing the Results

1. Tell the students to put their animals and materials away.

2. Have the teams discuss their results and write down their conclusions.

3. Remind the teams to save the "Animal Behavior Experiment" sheets as evidence for the reports each team will present during the next session, "The Scientific Convention."

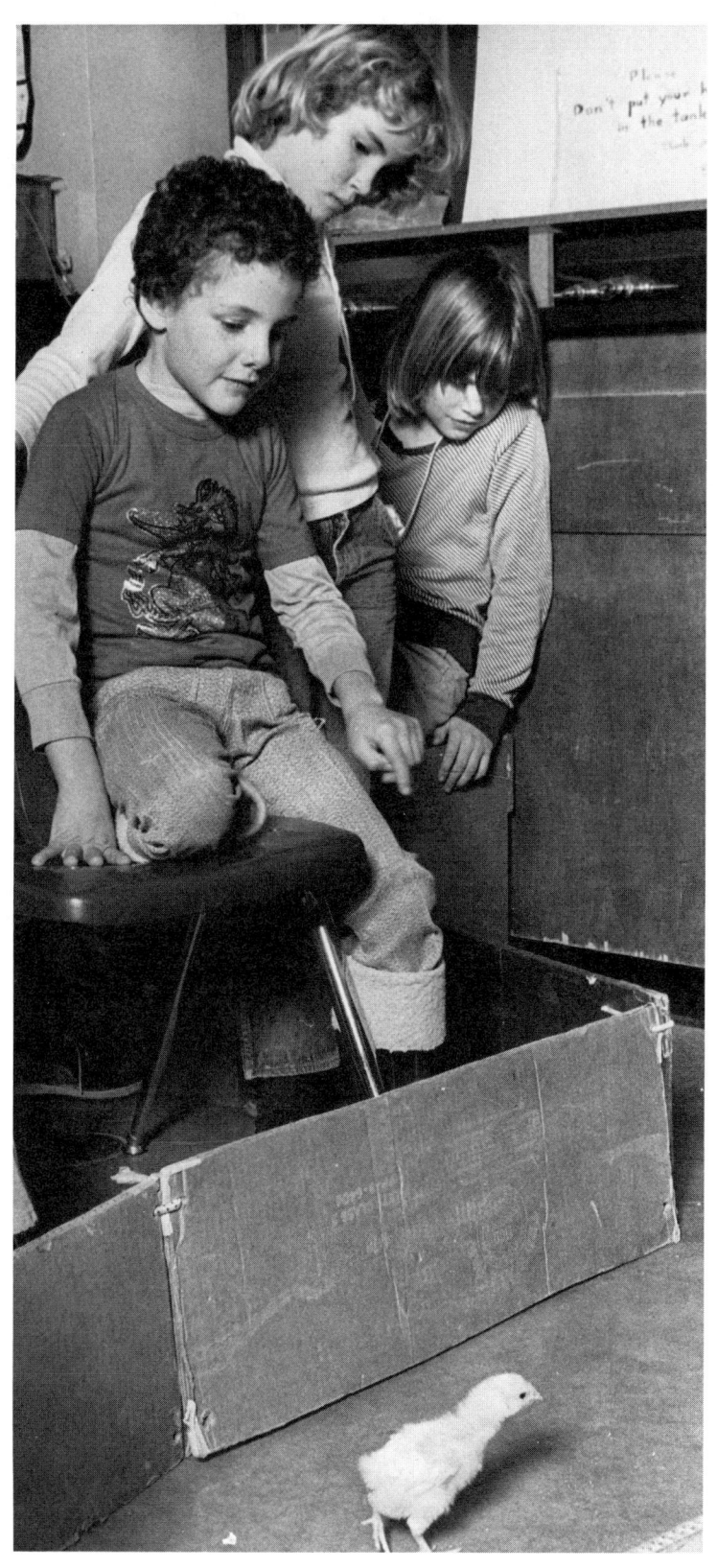

Session 5: The Scientific Convention

Overview

This group session can provide a dynamic forum for learning about the importance of objectivity in reporting observations, experimenter bias, fair experiments, and respect for other points of view.

Students vary in their ability to speak out in an open discussion. To promote dialogue, encourage a tone of mutual respect and support among the group. Take advantage of the students' interest in animal behavior to stimulate a lively exchange of information.

Time Frame

Getting Started   5 minutes
Convention in Session   40 minutes

What You Need

For each team:
- ☐ Student sheets from previous sessions, "Animal Behavior Experiment"

Getting Ready

To formulate an agenda for the convention, list the sequence of team reports on the board. If some experiments are similar or related, group them together to encourage students to make comparisons of methods and results.

Introducing the Convention

1. Explain the purpose of a scientific convention:

Scientists gather at large meetings to present and evaluate research, to share ideas, and to address controversial issues in science. The meetings are generally exciting. Scientists look forward to discussing new ideas and information.

2. Point out that the goal of the session is to share information. The participants should be attentive and polite so everyone receives a fair hearing.

3. Remind the teams to make use of their data sheets as evidence to support their conclusions. The teams may also decide to demonstrate the equipment and methods used in their experiments.

Convention in Session

1. Mention that each team's report is to last no more than five minutes.

2. Ask the first team to describe their experiment and summarize the results. Suggest that the presentations be short speeches rather than data read directly from their "Animal Behavior Experiment" sheets.

3. At the end of each report, call for comments and questions from the audience. The following questions may be helpful in stimulating discussion: "How well did the team avoid disturbing the animal subject?" "What did the team do to ensure the well-being of the animal?" "Was the experiment a *fair test*?"

4. Encourage students who weren't on the reporting team to offer additional information from their own findings.

5. In the case of conflicting results, ask the students to suggest reasons why two valid experiments might produce different conclusions.

Going Further

1. *Observations at Home*: Suggest that your students record their observations of a pet or a family member, such as a younger sibling. Remind students that good observers avoid disturbing their subjects. Wild birds and insects make particularly interesting subjects to study, so gardens and backyards are good sites for observation.

2. *More Experiments:* Schedule a future session for teams to revise and improve their experiments. Allow enough planning time to enable the students to gather additional materials and organisms. Some teams may want to swap experiments. Compare the results of these "repeat" experiments with the findings of the original research teams.

3. *Humane Guidelines:* As a class project, generate a list of guidelines for humane treatment of animals. In its final form, this list can be posted or displayed in the classroom.

4. Encourage your students to see the film "Never Cry Wolf," which chronicles the adventures of a biologist studying the behavior of wolves.

One student in a junior high class conducted a science fair project. He set out to map and define the territory covered by the neighborhood dog on its daily excursions. At various times during the week, he followed the dog carefully and recorded the route, range, and all "stops." He also kept a record of any interactions with other dogs along the route. If you and/or any of your students come up with ideas like this, let us hear about them!

Small Animal Resource Guide

The small animals suggested in this unit display an interesting variety of behaviors and are easily acquired from pet stores, bait shops, biological supply houses, and the out-of-doors. The following pages contain brief summaries of the care and feeding of a number of small animals, as well as possible questions to investigate in animal experiments.

Guppies and Gambusia

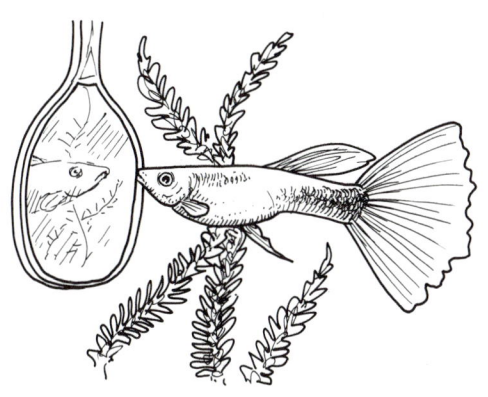

Food:
Fish food available from pet stores, small worms and insects.

Housing:
1–5 gallon, clear plastic or glass container to enable students to observe fish through the sides.

Care:
Place the guppies or gambusia in tap water that has been left to stand overnight to remove chlorine. Don't overfeed or water will become cloudy. Water temperature, 70–80°F (20–27°C).

Questions to Investigate:
Where do guppies swim when frightened?
Are guppies attracted by mirrors?
Do guppies prefer light or dark areas of water?
Do guppies prefer the top, bottom, or middle of the tank?

Crayfish

Food:
Crayfish will eat a great variety of things, including insects, worms, meat, pellet fish food, and aquatic plants.

Housing:
Plastic dishpans or similar containers with sides at least eight inches high to prevent animals from escaping.

Care:
Place the crayfish in tap water that has been left to stand overnight to remove chlorine. Shallow water, large surface area, and cool temperature, 65–75°F (18–24°C), to enhance the exchange of oxygen.
Feed in a separate container to prevent fouling of water.

Questions to Investigate:
Are crayfish attracted by bright colors?
Do crayfish prefer light or dark areas?
What causes a crayfish to swim backwards?
How do crayfish locate their food?

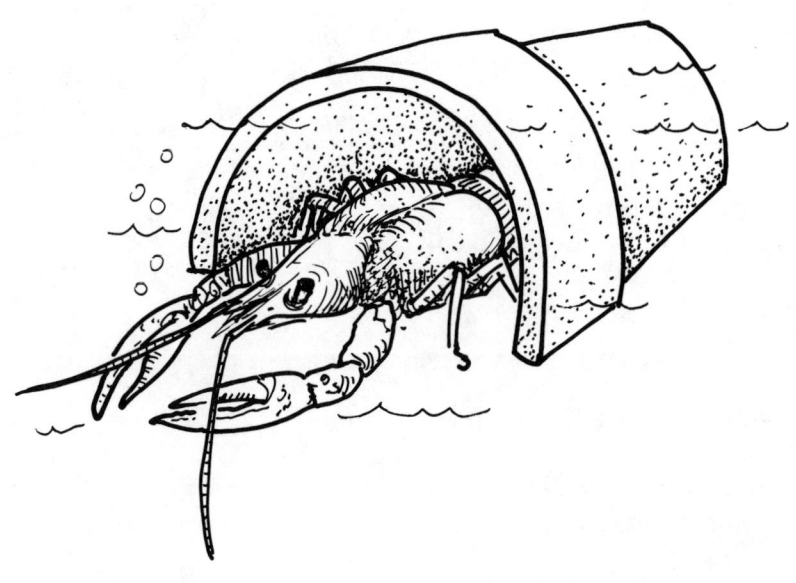

Milkweed Bugs

Food:
Milkweed plants, or shelled, unsalted sunflower seeds. Milkweed bug kits are available from biological supply companies.

Housing:
2–5 gallon aquarium with lid

Care:
Cover the bottom of the container with a thin layer of dry sand or soil, and add a few twigs. Add water to a piece of cotton placed in a small plastic lid.

Questions to Investigate:
On what surfaces can a milkweed bug hang upside down?
How do milkweed bugs react to air currents?
Are milkweed bugs attracted to or repelled by certain colors of light?
When placed in a box, will milkweed bugs prefer the edges or the center?

Isopods (Sowbugs and Pillbugs)

Food:
Isopods eat dead leaves, potato, lettuce, apple.

Housing:
Plastic sweater box, small bucket, metal coffee can.

Care:
Add several inches of moist soil containing dead leaves and twigs.
Keep container loosely covered and sprinkle with water periodically to keep the soil moist.

Questions to Investigate:
What kinds of plants do isopods avoid?
Are isopods attracted by dark areas?
Which moves faster, a pillbug or a sowbug?
Do isopods prefer dry or moist surfaces?

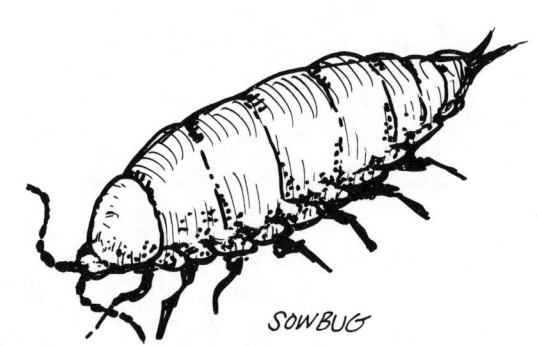
SOWBUG

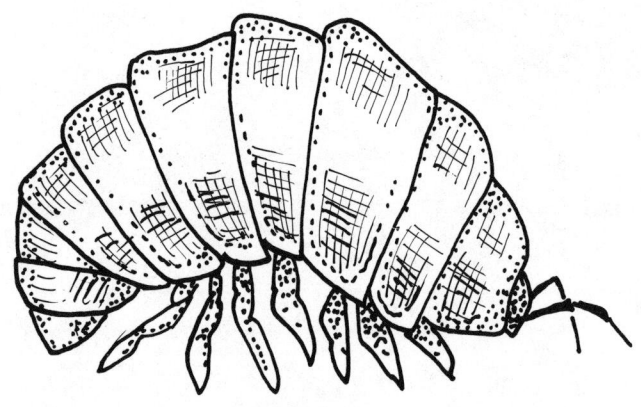
PILLBUG

Crickets

Food:
Powdered cereal or dog food, moist carrot, apple, or potato.

Housing:
Plastic sweater boxes with lids make good temporary containers. To establish a breeding colony use a 10-gallon aquarium with lid.

Care:
Add water to a piece of cotton placed in a small plastic lid. Moist soil or sand placed in a shallow container at one end of the cage will attract the females to lay eggs.
Add crumpled paper or parts of egg cartons for shelter.
Temperature 80–85°F (27–30°C).

Questions to Investigate:
What makes a cricket chirp?
Are male crickets more active than females?
What foods or things do crickets avoid?
Do crickets jump farther when they are warmer?

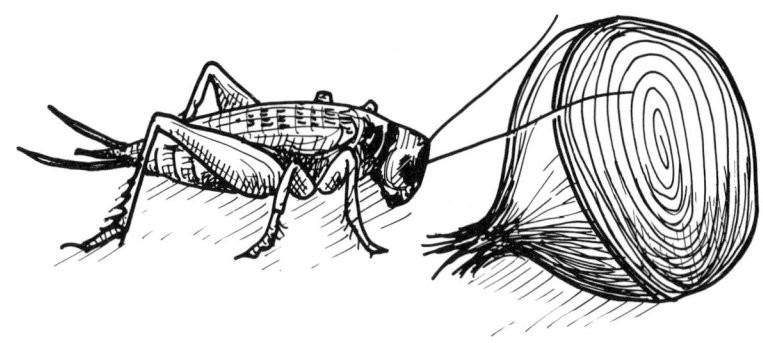

Grain Beetles and Mealworms

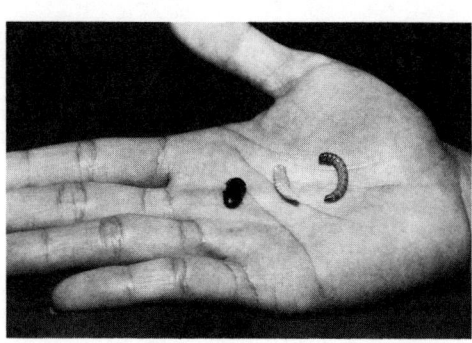

Food:
  Bran and moist pieces of potato or apple.

Housing:
  Plastic sweater box or bucket with lid.

Care:
  The bran should be several inches deep. Lay pieces of potato across the surface of the bran, and cover with a paper towel.

Questions to Investigate:
  When put on a slanted surface, which way will a mealworm travel?
  Do mealworms burrow or hide in materials other than bran?
  What surfaces will a grain beetle avoid?
  Do grain beetles have a preference for color?

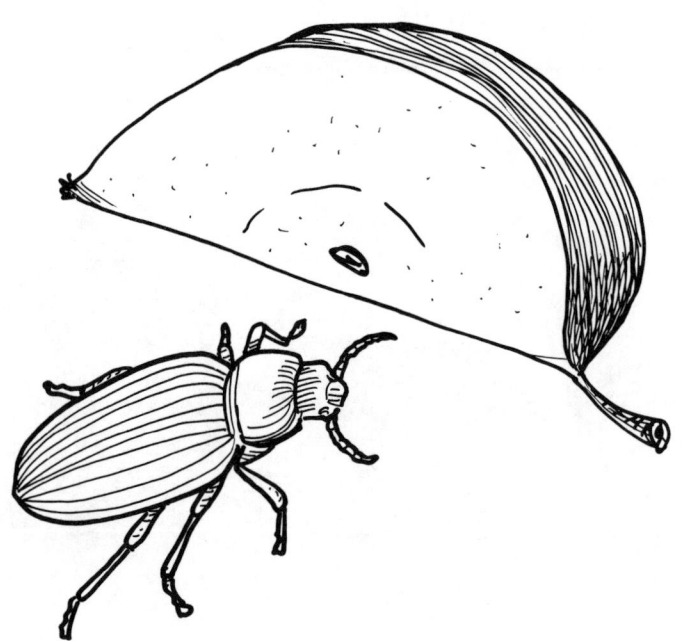

Lady Beetles (Ladybugs)

Food:
Small insects such as aphids.

Housing:
2-gallon aquarium with lid.

Care:
Cover the bottom with soil, and provide leafy twigs.
Provide water by lightly misting the container about every other day.

Questions to Investigate:
What stimulates a ladybug to fly?
Do ladybugs get together in groups when it is cold?
On what surface will a ladybug move fastest?
What color background does a ladybug prefer?
Do ladybugs "play dead" when disturbed?

Butterfly And Moth Larvae

(Painted Lady Butterfly, Tobacco Horn Worm, Greater Wax Moth)

Food:
Larvae are available in kits with food from a number of biological supply companies. If the organisms are collected in the field, bring in leaves from the plant on which the larvae are found.

Housing:
A cardboard shoe box is spacious enough for several larvae. Cut a large window in the lid of the box and tape clear plastic wrap over the opening. Punch small holes in the sides of the box for ventilation or cut a window and cover with netting. Cover the bottom of the box with a paper towel. Refer to drawing.

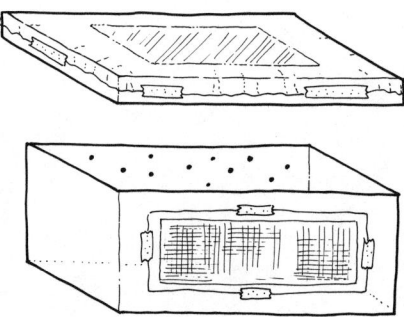

Care:
The butterfly and moth kits will come with instructions for care and housing.
Refer to *Creatures in the Classroom* for the care and feeding of a variety of species of butterflies and moths.

Questions to Investigate:
Do the larvae prefer to move up or down a slanted surface?
Are the larvae attracted by other larvae?
Do they move faster or slower when it is windy?
Will they choose surfaces that are the same color as themselves?

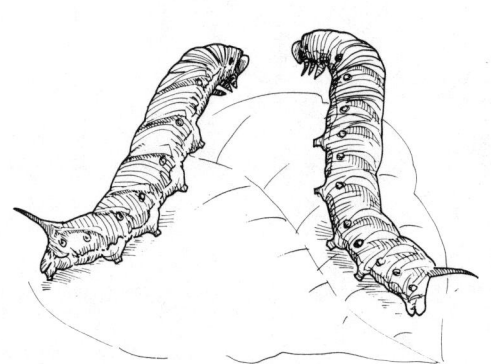

Garden Snails

Food:
Lettuce leaves, oatmeal, dry cereal, potato.

Housing:
5-gallon plastic bucket having a lid with a few holes

Care:
Cover the bottom with gravel.
Add some egg shell or oyster shell for calcium, and branches for climbing.
Mist the container every few days and remove moldy food.

Questions to Investigate:
How can you attract a snail so that it sticks its head out of its shell?
Which way will a snail choose to travel on a slanted surface?
Are snails attracted to light?
Will they avoid garlic, orange peels, hair, onion, salt, beer?

Where To Get Live Critters

There are many sources for live animals, so the following list is by no means exhaustive, and does not constitute a recommendation of one source over another. It is intended simply as a helpful starting point and resource.

Bassett Cricket Ranch
535 North Lover's Lane
Visalia, CA 93291 (209) 732-2738

Carolina Biological Supply Company
2700 York Road
Burlington, NC 27215 (919) 584-0381

Connecticut Valley Biological Supply Co.
82 Valley Road P.O. Box 326
Southampton, MA 01073 (800) 638-7748

Delta Education, Inc.
P.O. Box 915
Hudson, NH 03051-0915 (800) 258-1302

Fisher Scientific Company
4901 W. Lemoyne Street
Chicago, IL 60651 1(800) 621-4769

McKilligan Supply Corporation
435 Main Street
Johnson City, NY 13790 (607) 729-6511

Nasco
901 Janesville Avenue
Fort Atkinson, WI (800) 558-9595

Nasco West, Inc.
P.O. Box 3837
Modesto, CA 95352 (209) 529-6957

Science Kit and Boreal Labs
777 E. Park Drive
Tonawanda, NY 14150 (800) 828-7777

Ward's Natural Science Establishment
P.O. Box 92912
Rochester, NY 14692-9012 (800) 962-2660

Western Scientific Company
P.O. Box 681
West Sacramento, CA 95691 (916) 371-2705

Code of Practice on Use of Animals in Schools

This code of practice is recommended by the National Science Teachers Association for use throughout the United States by elementary, middle/junior high, and high school teachers and students. It applies to educational projects conducted and lessons taught, involving live organisms in schools or in school-related activities such as science fairs, science clubs, and science competitions.

The purpose of these guidelines is to enrich education by encouraging students to observe living organisms and to learn proper respect for life. The study of living organisms is essential for an understanding of living processes. This study must be coupled with the observance of humane animal care and treatment.

I. Care and Responsibility for Animals in the Classroom

A. A teacher must have a clear understanding of and a strong commitment to the responsible care of living animals before making any decision to use live animals for educational study. Preparation for the use of live animals should include acquisition of knowledge on care appropriate to the species being used including housing, food, exercise, and the appropriate placement of the animals at the conclusion of the study.
B. Teachers should try to assure that living animals entering the classroom are healthy and free of transmissible disease or other problems that may endanger human health. Not all species are appropriate. Wild animals are not appropriate because they may carry parasites or serious diseases.
C. Maintaining good health and providing optimal care based on an understanding of the life habits of each species used is of primary importance. Animal quarters shall be spacious, shall avoid overcrowding, and shall be sanitary. Handling shall be gentle. Food shall be appropriate to the animal's normal diet and of sufficient quantity and balance to maintain a good standard of nutrition at all times. No animal shall be allowed less than the optimum maintenance level of nutrition. Clean drinking water shall always be available. Adequate provision for care shall be made at all times including vacation times.
D. All aspects of animal care and treatment shall be supervised by a qualified ADULT WHO IS KNOWLEDGEABLE ABOUT RESEARCH METHODS, BIOLOGY, CARE, AND HUSBANDRY OF THE SPECIES BEING STUDIED.
E. Supervisors and students should be familiar with *literature on care and handling* of living organisms. Practical training in these techniques is encouraged.
F. Adequate plans should be made to *control possible unwanted breedings* of the species during the project period.
G. Appropriate plans should be made for future care of animals at the conclusion of the study.
H. As a general rule, laboratory-bred animals should not be released into the wild as they may disturb the natural ecology of the environment.
I. On rare occasions it may be necessary to sacrifice an animal for educational purposes. This shall be done only in a manner accepted and approved by the American Veterinary Association, by a person experienced in these techniques, and at the discretion of the teacher. It should not be done in the presence of immature or young students who may be upset by witnessing such a procedure. Maximum efforts should be made to study as many biological principles as possible from a single animal.
J. The procurement, care, and use of animals must comply with existing local, state, and federal regulations.

II. Experimental Studies of Animals in the Classroom

A. When biological procedures involving living organisms are called for, every effort should be made to use plants or invertebrate animals when possible.
B. No experimental procedure shall be attempted on mammals, birds, reptiles, amphibians, or fish that causes the animal unnecessary pain or discomfort.
C. It is recommended that preserved vertebrate specimens be used for dissections.
D. Students shall not perform dissection surgery on vertebrate animals except under direct supervision of a qualified biomedical scientist or trained adult supervisor.
E. *Experimental procedures* including the use of pathogens, ionizing radiation, toxic chemicals, and chemicals producing birth defects must be under the supervision of a biomedical scientist or an adult trained in the specific techniques. Such procedures should be done in appropriate laboratory facilities that adhere to safety guidelines.
F. *Behavior studies should use only reward* (such as providing food) and not punishment in training programs. When food is used as a reward, it should not be withheld for more than 12 hours.
G. If embryos are subjected to invasive or potentially damaging experimental manipulation, the embryo must be destroyed prior to hatching. If normal embryos are hatched, provisions must be made for their care and maintenance.

III. Research Investigations Involving Vertebrate Animals

The National Science Teachers Association recognizes that an exceptionally talented student may wish to conduct research in the biological or medical sciences and endorses procedures for student research as follows:
A. Protocols of extracurricular projects involving animals should be reviewed in advance of the start of the work by a qualified adult supervisor.
B. Preferably, extracurricular projects should be carried out in an approved area of the school or research facility.
C. The project should be carried out with the utmost regard for the humane care and treatment of the animals involved in the project.

—*Adopted by the NSTA Board of Directors in July 1985.*

References

Dewsbury, D.A., *Comparative Animal Behavior.* New York, McGraw-Hill Book Co., 1978.

Elementary Science Study, *Teacher's Guide for Crayfish.* New York, McGraw-Hill Book Co., 1969.

Elementary Science Study, *Teacher's Guide for Behavior of Mealworms.* New York, McGraw-Hill Book Co., 1966.

Hansell, M.H., Aitken, J.J. *Experimental Animal Behavior: A Selection of Laboratory Exercises.* London, Blackie & Son, Ltd., 1977.

Multnomah County Intermediate Education District, *Creatures in the Classroom.* Portland, Oregon, 1976.

> This comprehensive resource book is available from:
>
> Curriculum Department
> Multnomah County Education District
> P.O. Box 301039
> Portland, OR 97230
> (503) 257-1630

National Science Teachers Association, "Code of Practice on Use of Animals in Schools," in *the Science Teacher,* Washington, D.C., January 1986.

Outdoor Biology Instructional Strategies, *Isopods.* Developed by and available from the Lawrence Hall of Science, Berkeley, California. Delta Publishing Co., Nashua, New Hampshire, 1976.

"Rules of the 35th International Science and Engineering Fair (1984)," Science Service, Inc., 1719 N Street N.W., Washington, D.C. 20036.

Summary Outlines

Session 1: The Animal Corral

Animal Observations
1. Have students sit down in chairs around corral. Pick up first animal gently.
2. Explain that the term *behavior* means everything an animal does.
3. Have student volunteer place the animal in corral; students take turns describing behavior.
4. After 5 minutes, return animal to cage.
5. With students still seated around corral, write "Observations" on board and ask students what it means. [Based on what we can perceive with our senses]
6. List 5 to 10 student observations. Accept all suggestions.
7. Then insert an *assumption* of your own, such as "the animal wants to get out." Explain why this is not a direct observation.
8. Erase the assumption and ask students to suggest an observed action.
9. Have students check over the list in this light, and put parentheses around entries that are not observations.
10. Introduce the term *anthropomorphism*. Give an example and have students suggest others.

More Observations
1. Ask a volunteer to add another animal to the corral. Have students quietly describe the animal's actions.
2. After removing animal from corral, begin a new list of observations.
3. Ask if there are any assumptions or anthropomorphisms.
4. If the two animals are compatible, place them in corral together and have students observe a few more minutes.
5. Stimulate discussion by asking questions to compare and contrast behavior, location, etc.
6. Have class check that conclusions drawn are based on direct observations.
7. Students who handled animals should wash hands with soap and water.
8. Ask students to bring in non-harmful materials from home, such as food, shelter, toys, etc., to add to corral environment.

Humane Treatment of Animals
1. Explain that there are laws protecting animals. Ask, "Why do you suppose people have to make these laws?"
2. Introduce the term *humane*, ask students how they can be humane to classroom animals, and list their responses on a large sheet of paper.

Session 2: Stimulus and Response

Stimulus and Response
1. As students sit around corral, explain they will be like a team of biologists observing how an animal reacts to environmental changes.
2. Introduce stimulus and response by making a loud noise or use another unusual action to surprise the class. Ask students how they reacted.
3. Explain a *stimulus* as anything to which an organism reacts (the loud noise) and a *response* is how the organism reacts (the students' surprised reactions).
4. Ask students to examine the corral environment and name potential stimuli.
5. Show students various objects that may be added to the corral as stimuli for the animal.
6. Ask volunteer to put one animal in corral, then students take turns describing the animal's actions.
7. Let class choose which stimulus to add first, have volunteer add it to corral, and list observations.
8. Other volunteers add new objects, one at a time. Observe animal's response for several minutes before removing object and adding a new one. After about 10 minutes volunteer removes animal from corral.
9. Ask how the animal responded to the volunteer, which stimulus attracted it most, and what qualities of the object might have attracted the animal.
10. Have volunteer remove stimulus objects from corral and add another animal. Repeat stimulus/response tests and record student observations.
11. If the two animals are compatible, return first animal to corral and have students observe interactions.

Discussion

1. Ask students to consider data when comparing actions of the two animals.
2. Encourage sharing of ideas about why certain actions might benefit a wild animal.
3. Point out that it is often hard to identify which stimuli cause certain behaviors, and hard to determine the exact use or value of a particular response. Scientists come up with ideas about this to make a *hypothesis* they can investigate.
4. Guide the students in coming up with hypotheses to explain some animal behavior.
5. Ask for ideas on how the behavior of a wild animal could be studied and recorded.
6. Announce that they will conduct their own investigations in future sessions.

Session 3: Small Critters in Action

Describing Actions

1. Tell students they'll be investigating behavior of a small animal and have them re-define *behavior*.
2. Introduce the animals and explain where you got them, without revealing information they can discover on their own.
3. Explain procedure of adding stimulus objects to container to see response.
4. Distribute "Observing Animal Behavior" sheet and clipboards for each student to record observations.
5. Divide class into teams of 4 and review stimulus objects.
6. Tell students to introduce one stimulus at a time, and to carefully observe and record. Remind students about humane treatment.
7. Give each team a container with 1 or 2 animals, and tell them they have about 15 minutes to test responses to stimuli.
8. After 15 minutes, collect containers and animals.

Discussing Observations

1. Ask students to report which stimuli seem to influence behavior. List on board.
2. Referring to observations, ask if any are *anthropomorphisms* or *assumptions*.

Planning Experiments
1. Explain that you'll help students design an animal behavior experiment:
    a. Choose one stimuli and a topic.
    b. Narrow it down to a hypothesis that can be tested in 25 minutes.
    c. Identify the choices for the animal.
    d. Identify what you will observe and record.
    e. Describe how to make it a *fair test*.
2. Choosing a realistic topic and a clear plan are crucial. Emphasize importance of good advance planning.
3. Suggest other experiments, perhaps consulting the "Small Animal Resource Guide" in this book or listing possible variables on board.
4. Distribute "Animal Behavior Experiment" sheets and encourage teams to spend 10 minutes planning and filling in first two items.
5. Have one or two teams describe and discuss their plans with the class. Encourage constructive suggestions.
6. Collect team plans for your review before next session.

Session 4: Team Experiments

Getting Started
1. Stress need for teamwork. Have teams select a Recorder, Materials Manager, Animal Manager, and Assistant Animal Manager.
2. Return the "Animal Behavior Experiment" data sheets to team Recorders and remind students to assist Recorder in making observations.
3. Have teams get materials and begin their experiments, to last no more than 25 minutes.

Experimenting
1. Circulate and assist as needed, encouraging students to be precise in describing their observations.
2. Remind students to avoid interfering with the animals during the experiment, and to give animals a few minutes to respond to stimuli.
3. At midpoint, remind teams of the time limit, and stress the important of recording **all** results.

Analyzing the Results
1. Have students put animals and materials away.
2. Have teams discuss results and write down conclusions.
3. Remind teams to save their data sheets for use in the reports they present in the next session.

Session 5: The Scientific Convention

Introducing the Convention
1. Explain the purpose of a scientific convention as gatherings of scientists to evaluate research, share ideas, and address issues.
2. The goal of this session is to share information. Everyone should be attentive and polite.
3. Remind teams to use their data sheets as evidence to support their conclusions.

Convention in Session
1. Mention that each team's report is to last no more than five minutes.
2. Ask first team to describe their experiment and summarize results in a short speech, rather than a straight reading of the data sheet.
3. After each report, call for comments and questions, and stimulate discussion as needed by asking questions.
4. Encourage other students to comment if they have relevant information from their own experiments.
5. If conflicting results surface, ask students to suggest reasons why two valid experiments could produce different results.

NAME: _____

OBSERVING ANIMAL BEHAVIOR

Name of Animal: _____

List the stimuli you used and the animal's responses:

Object or Stimulus	Response

RECORDER: _____
OTHER TEAM MEMBERS: _____
_____
_____

ANIMAL BEHAVIOR EXPERIMENT

Name of Animal:

1. What is your hypothesis?

2. Describe your experiment:

3. Record your observations:

4. What are your conclusions?

5. How did you make sure the experiment was a **fair test?**

6. Ideas for improving the experiment:

7. On the back of this paper sketch your experimental setup.

Notes

Notes